I Can Make EXCITING ELECTRONICS

by Kristina A. Holzweiss
and Amy Barth

TABLE OF CONTENTS

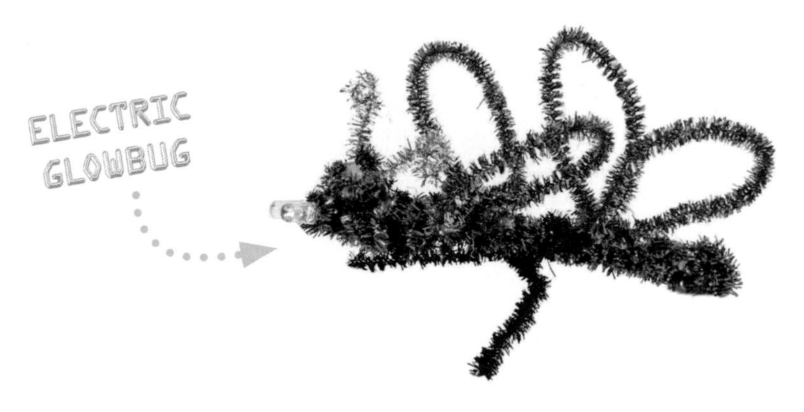
ELECTRIC
GLOWBUG

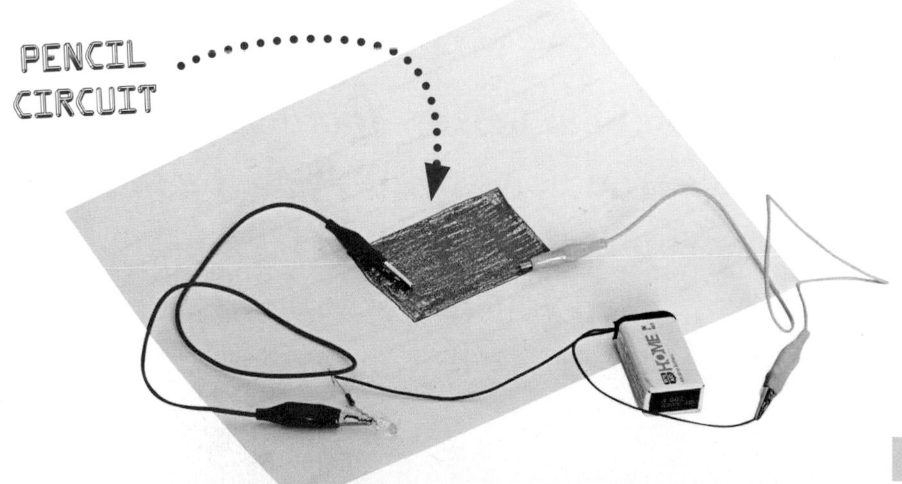
PENCIL
CIRCUIT

ARE YOU A MAKER?

Makers are inventors, artists, and builders. In this book, you will learn how to make three exciting electronics: a fluttering butterfly, an electric glowbug, and a pencil circuit.

These projects look very different from each other. But they have something in common—they are all powered by **electricity**.

Anyone can be a maker. You don't need fancy tools. You don't need to be a computer whiz. Are you creative and up for an adventure? Then you've got what it takes. Let's get started!

ELECTRIC
GLOWBUG
FLUTTERING
BUTTERFLY
PENCIL CIRCUIT

MAKING CAN HAPPEN ANYWHERE!

You don't need a workshop to be a maker. You can make things in a classroom or on your kitchen floor. Project materials can be found around the house or at a craft shop.

You will need an adult's help with some steps. Like all inventors, you will try out your electronics. Then you will change your designs to make them even better.

PROJECT 1

YOU CAN MAKE A FLUTTERING BUTTERFLY

Butterflies are flying insects. They have big, colorful wings. Butterflies flap their wings to help them fly through the air.

You can build a butterfly machine that moves its wings. Your butterfly will be powered by electricity.

HOW A FLUTTERING BUTTERFLY WORKS

BATTERY
The battery provides electricity. The electricity flows through the wires, making them spin.

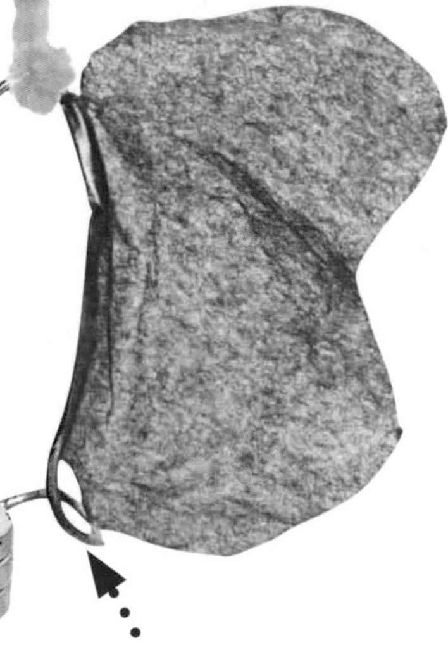

MAGNETS
Neodymium (nee-oh-**di**-mee-um) magnets connect to the battery and wings. The magnets direct the flow of electricity through the wire.

WIRE
The frames of the butterfly's wings are made of copper wire. Copper is a type of metal. Copper is a good **conductor**. That means electricity travels easily through it.

Electricity happens naturally all around us. Lightning bolts are made from electricity. Static electricity is created when objects rub against each other. Static electricity gives you a small shock when you touch a doorknob. It also makes your hair stand up when you take off your winter hat.

DISCOVER MORE ABOUT

ELECTRIC CURRENTS

Current electricity is electricity that moves from one place to another. The current travels through a conductor. That is a material that allows electricity to flow freely. Static electricity is energy that has gathered in one place. It does not move.

YOU WILL NEED

- ☐ Three neodymium magnets (bought online or at a home improvement store)
- ☐ AA battery
- ☐ 12–16 inches of solid, bendable copper wire
- ☐ Needle-nose pliers
- ☐ Scissors
- ☐ Tissue paper
- ☐ Clear tape
- ☐ Two 2-inch pieces of pipe cleaner

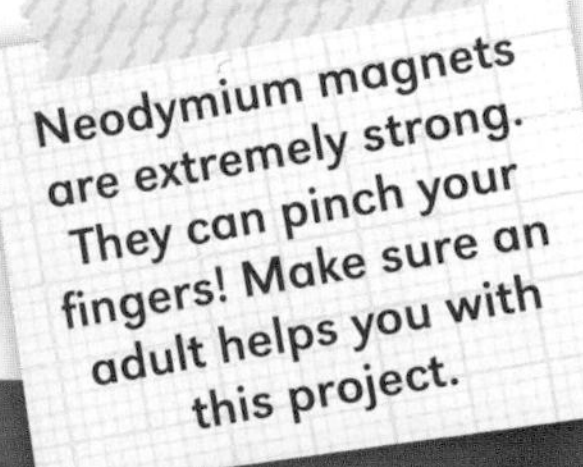

Neodymium magnets are extremely strong. They can pinch your fingers! Make sure an adult helps you with this project.

INSTRUCTIONS

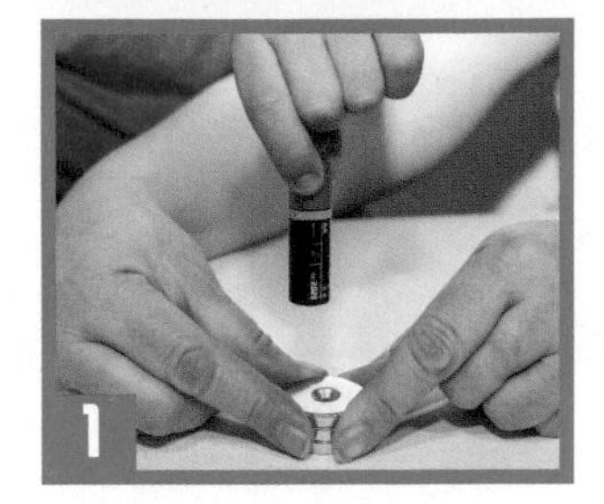

1

Ask an adult for help stacking the magnets on a flat surface. Place the negative (flat) end of the battery on top of the magnets.

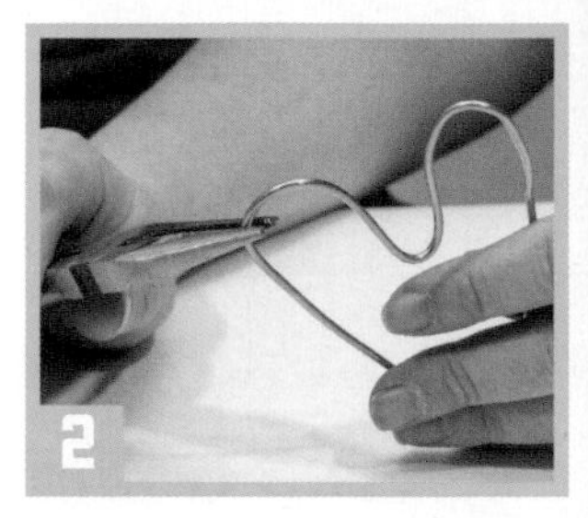

2

Ask an adult for help bending the copper wire in half. Use the pliers to bend the wire into a heart shape.

Position the heart on top of the battery. Bend the bottom ends of the heart so they form a circle that can spin around the magnets. Carefully remove the heart from the battery.

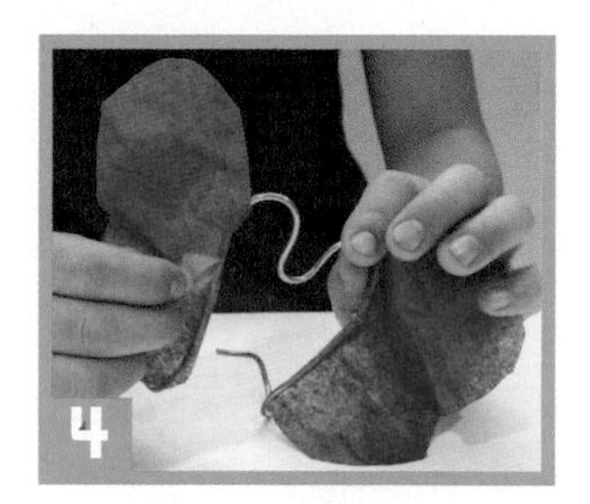

Cut two small wings out of the tissue paper. Use tape to attach one wing to each side of the heart.

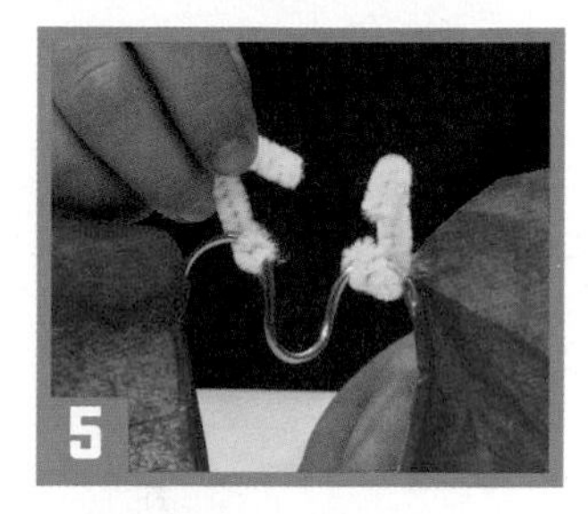

Twist the pipe cleaners to make spirals. Attach them to the top of the heart to create antennae.

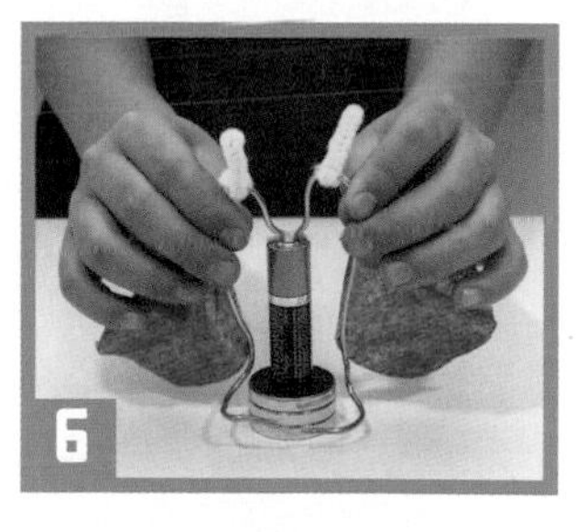

Balance the butterfly on top of the battery.

MAKE IT MOVE

Give the butterfly a nudge and watch it spin! Adjust the loop if the butterfly does not spin freely. Watch out—as your butterfly spins, the copper wire can get hot.

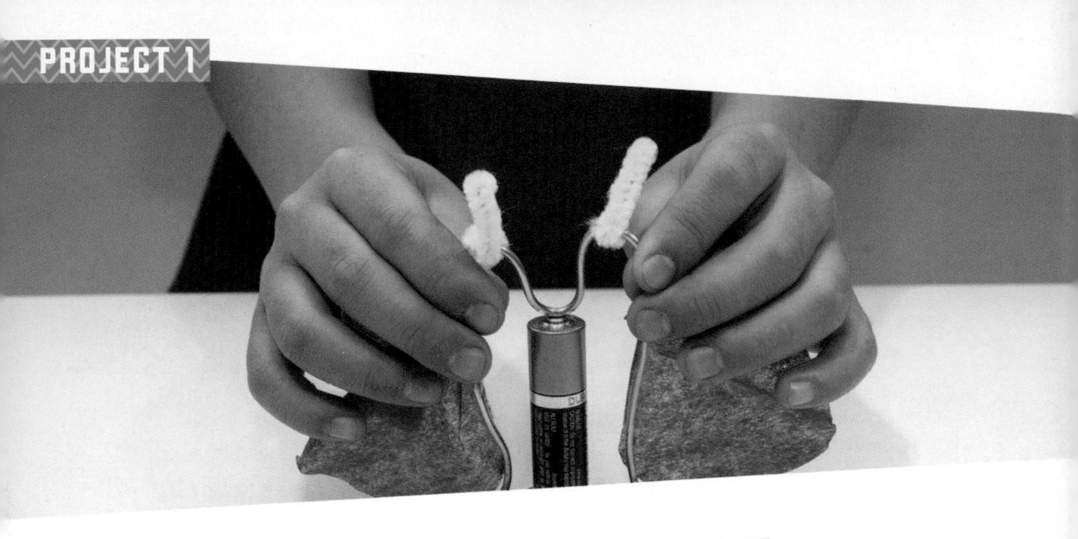

TEST IT

Set a timer for 10 seconds. Count the number of times your butterfly spins. Is it spinning quickly or slowly?

CHANGE IT

- Turn the battery upside down. Does that change the direction in which the wings spin?
- What happens if you use fewer magnets?
- What happens if you use a different gauge (thickness) of copper wire?

PROJECT 2

YOU CAN MAKE AN ELECTRIC GLOWBUG

A glowworm is a small insect that glows in the dark. It can have a green or yellow light at the end of its tail. A firefly is another type of insect that glows. Chemicals in the insects' bodies produce light. You can use electricity to make your own glowbug!

HOW AN ELECTRIC GLOWBUG WORKS

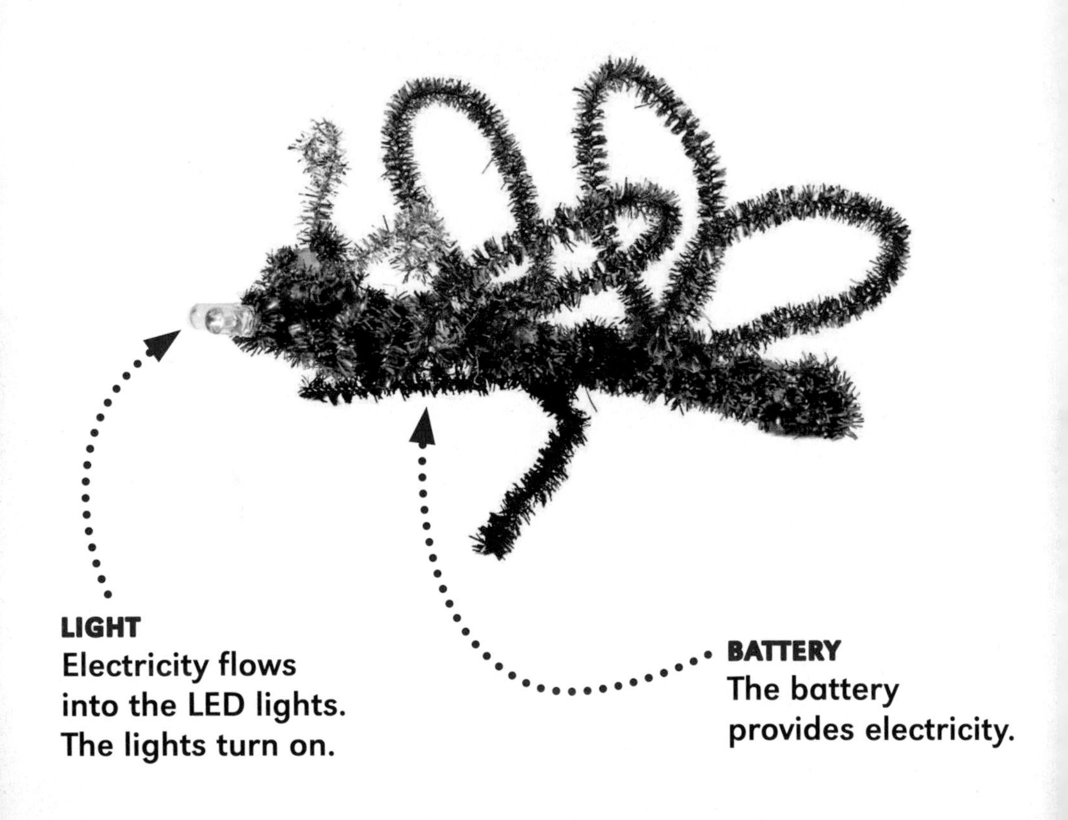

LIGHT
Electricity flows into the LED lights. The lights turn on.

BATTERY
The battery provides electricity.

There are many types of lights. Some people use incandescent light bulbs. These bulbs are usually made of glass. They have a small metal wire on the inside. An electric current passes through the metal, heating it up. That produces light. After many hours of use, the metal wears down. The light bulb burns out.

DISCOVER MORE ABOUT

LED LIGHTS

You are using a different type of light in this project. LED stands for light emitting diode. These light bulbs last longer than other bulbs. And they use less energy. LEDs do not burn out like incandescent bulbs. They slowly get dimmer over time.

YOU WILL NEED

- ☐ CR2032 3V coin battery
- ☐ Two LED lights
- ☐ Electrical tape
- ☐ Craft stick
- ☐ Pipe cleaners

INSTRUCTIONS

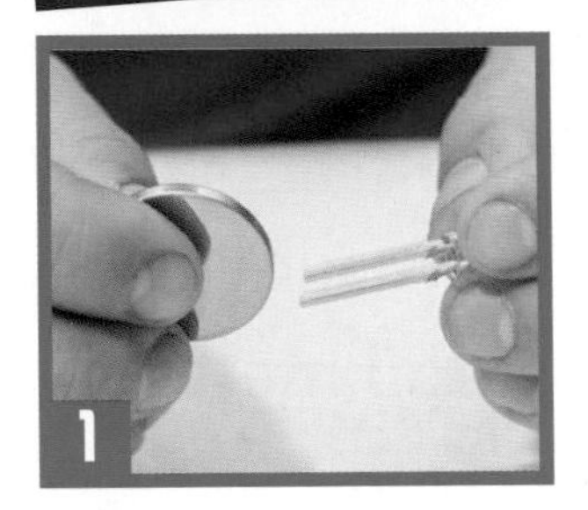

Place the battery between the two ends of one LED light. The longer end should touch the positive side of the battery. The shorter end should touch the negative side.

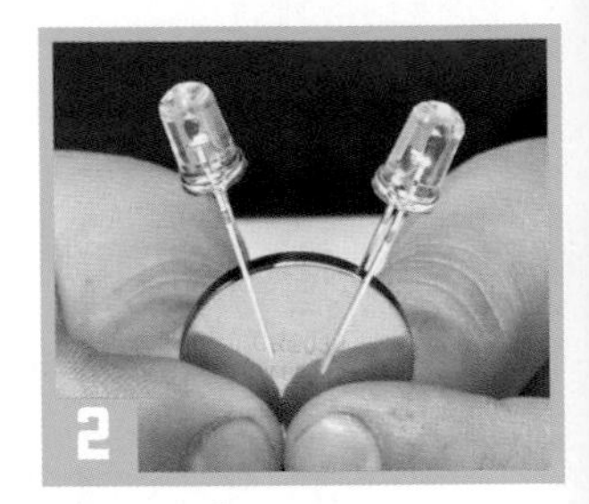

Slide the battery between the two ends of the second LED. Make sure everything matches up as in Step 1.

MAKE IT GLOW

Once the LED lights and battery are connected, the bug should light up. If it doesn't, you can "debug" the problem. You can try using another battery or other LED lights. Or try turning the battery around.

Wrap some tape around the LEDs and battery. This will be your glowbug's eyes.

Tape the "eyes" to the end of the craft stick.

Wrap pipe cleaners around the craft stick. This is the glowbug's body. Add other features, like feet and wings.

TEST IT

Take the bug to a dark place. Does it glow? Point your glowbug toward a wall. Is the light shining on the wall bright or dim?

CHANGE IT

- Try different color LED lights. Which glows the brightest?
- Use four LEDs to make a powerful bug.
- Use two batteries (one for each LED light). Does the bug glow brighter?

PROJECT 3

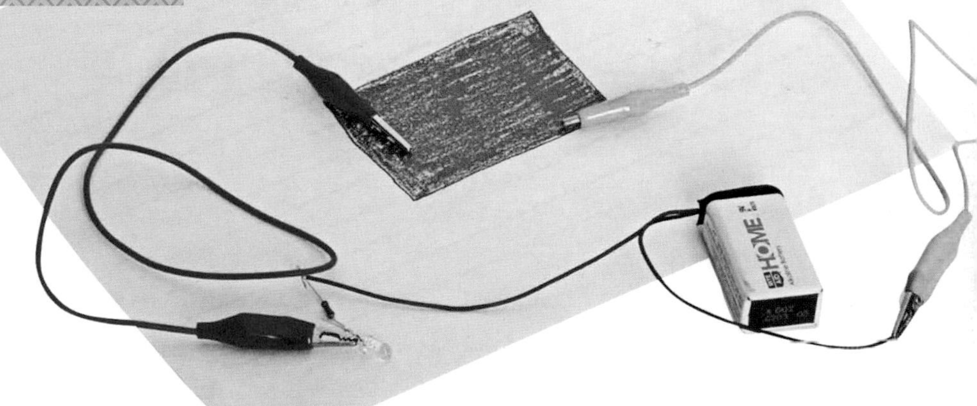

YOU CAN MAKE A PENCIL CIRCUIT

Most lights are powered by electricty from a battery or an electrical outlet. In both cases, the power flows through wires into a light bulb. But there are other creative ways to conduct electricity. You can even use a drawing to do it!

HOW A PENCIL CIRCUIT WORKS

CIRCUIT

You are making a closed circuit.

CONDUCTOR

Pencil lead is made of graphite. Graphite is a conductor.

LED BULB

The light is an electrical **load**. This is the part of your circuit that uses power.

RESISTOR

The **resistor** reduces the flow of the electrical current. Without it, the bulb would burn out.

BATTERY

The battery provides electricity.

An electrical circuit is a path that electricity flows along. All circuits have a power source, like a battery. Circuits are made of conductors, like metal wires. Conductors allow electricity to flow through them. Along the path is a load, like a light bulb. When everything is connected, it forms a circuit!

DISCOVER MORE ABOUT

OPEN & CLOSED CIRCUITS

A closed circuit is one in which the current can flow in an uninterrupted path. (An open circuit is when the path is broken.) In this project, the battery, snap connector, resistor, LED bulb, alligator cables, and your drawing are all linked together. That forms a closed circuit.

YOU WILL NEED

- ☐ ¼ watt 200 ohm resistor
- ☐ 3.2–3.4 LED bulb
- ☐ Wire stripper
- ☐ 9-volt snap connector
- ☐ Two double-ended alligator cables
- ☐ Soft drawing pencil (6B from an art supply shop is best)
- ☐ Plain white paper
- ☐ 9-volt battery

INSTRUCTIONS

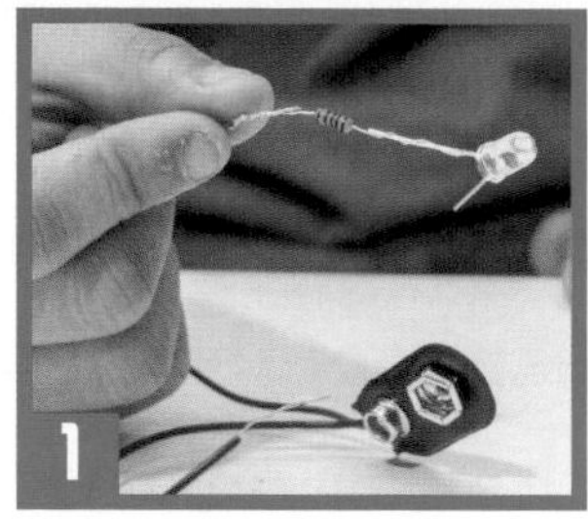

1

Ask an adult for help using the wire stripper. Strip half an inch of insulation off each end of the snap connector wire. Twist the end of the red wire to one end of the resistor. Twist the other end of the resistor on to the long end of the LED bulb.

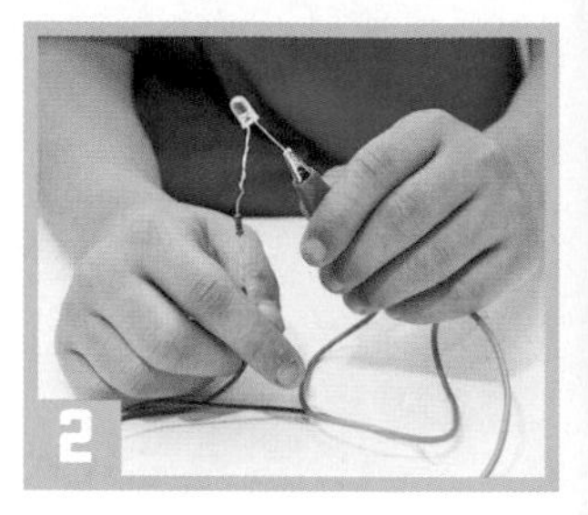

2

Clip one end of an alligator cable to the shorter end of the LED bulb.

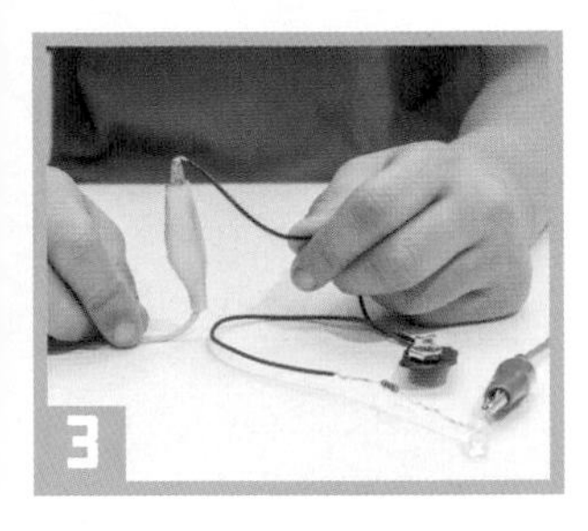
3

Clip one end of the other alligator cable to the negative (black) wire of the snap connector.

4

Draw a rectangle about 2 inches long and 1 inch wide on the piece of paper. Fill in the rectangle. Go over the drawing firmly—at least 15 times—to make it dark.

5

Connect the snap connector to the battery.

TURN IT ON

Touch the free ends of the alligator cables to the drawing. The light will not be superbright because the electricity flows through the graphite, which offers resistance.

TEST IT

Remove the end of one of the alligator cables from the drawing. Now the circuit is broken. The LED bulb should turn off. Press the end of the alligator cable onto your drawing to close the circuit. The light should turn back on.

CHANGE IT

- Try drawing a conductor that is a lot bigger or a lot smaller. Does size make a difference?

- Draw a conductor using a regular No. 2 pencil. Does it work as well as the soft drawing pencil?

MASTERS OF ELECTRICITY

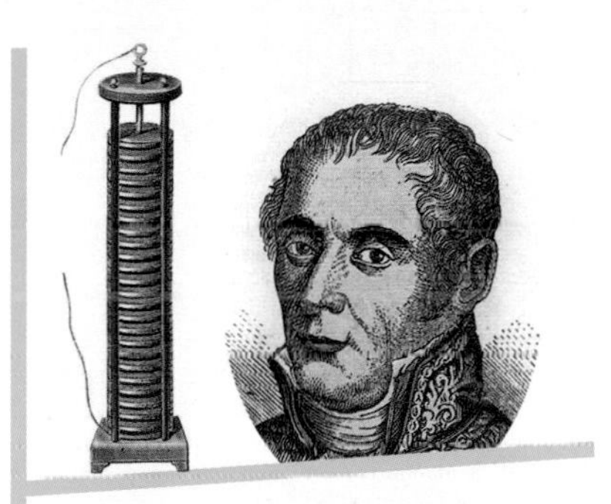

BENJAMIN FRANKLIN

Benjamin Franklin was born in America in 1706. He was one of the first people to study electricity. He captured lightning during a storm and discovered that it is a form of electricity. He also found that electricity can have a positive or negative charge.

ALESSANDRO VOLTA

Alessandro Volta was an Italian physicist born in 1745. He invented the first electric battery, which provided a continuous electric current. The volt, a unit used to measure the strength of an electrical current, was named after him in 1881.

THOMAS EDISON

Thomas Edison, an American inventor, was born in 1847. He did not invent the light bulb, but he figured out a way to make it better. In 1879, Edison built a light bulb that lasted for 13 hours—longer than any other at the time. His team also designed wiring and parts that turn lights on and off.

NIKOLA TESLA

Nikola Tesla was born in Croatia in 1856 and moved to the U.S. in 1884. Tesla invented alternate current (AC) circuits, which allow electricity to flow in different directions. This invention paved the way for more powerful electronics, like Tesla electric cars—named after Nikola Tesla.

PHILO FARNSWORTH

Philo Farnsworth, an American inventor, was born in 1906. Farnsworth improved early models of the television. He thought TVs should be powered by electricity, which would allow images to be displayed quickly. In 1927, Farnsworth showed off his model of the first electric television.

TIMELINE: ELECTRIC MOMENTS

Check out this timeline about some of the world's most electrifying moments.

600 BCE

Greek philosopher Thales of Miletus discovers static electricity.

1750s CE

Benjamin Franklin recognizes that electricity can carry positive and negative electric charges.

circa 1800

The first electric light is created by English scientist Humphry Davy.

The first electric battery is developed by Alessandro Volta.

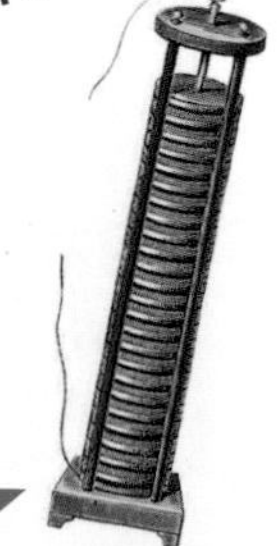

1821

The first electric motor is invented by English scientist Michael Faraday.

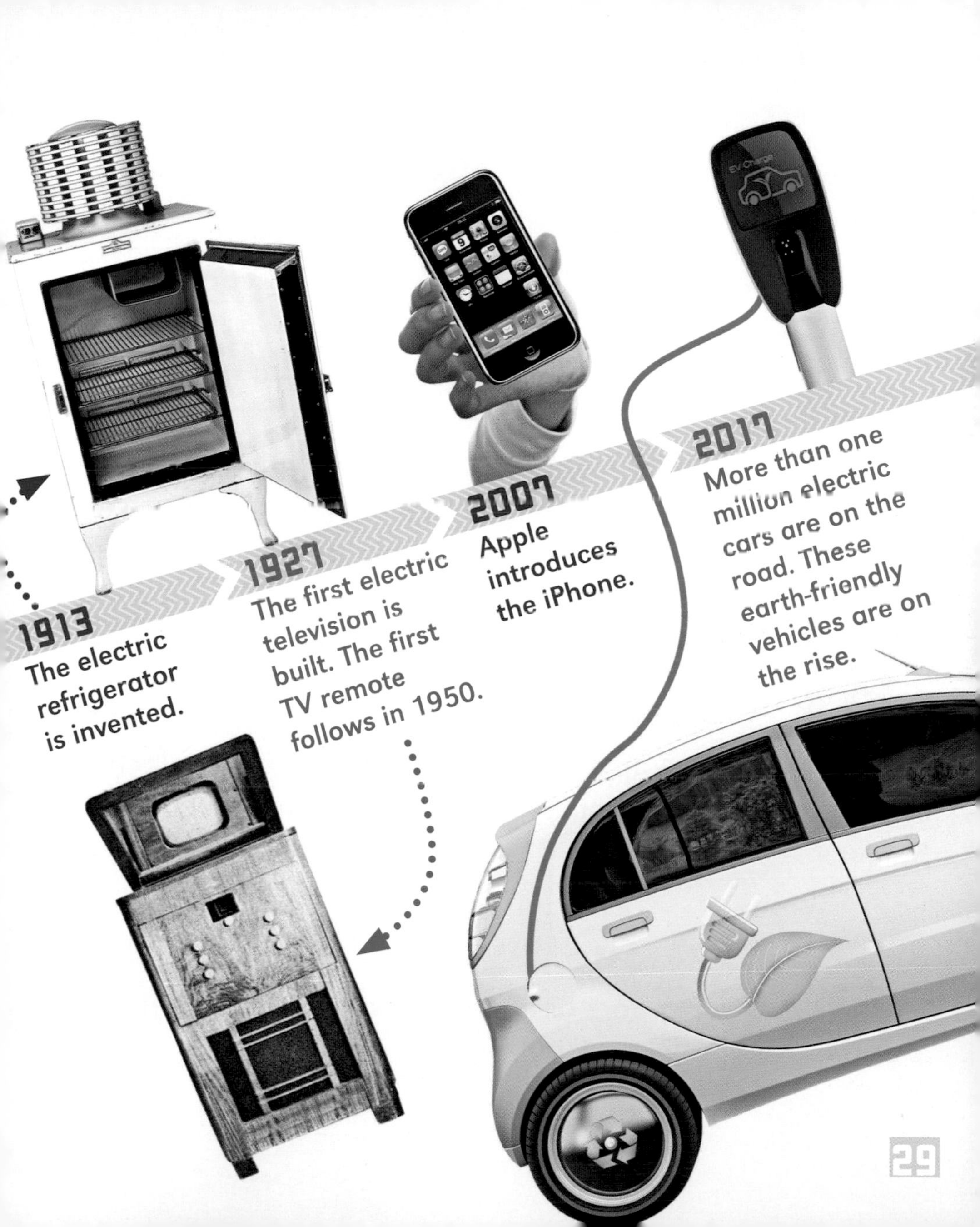

1913 The electric refrigerator is invented.

1927 The first electric television is built. The first TV remote follows in 1950.

2007 Apple introduces the iPhone.

2017 More than one million electric cars are on the road. These earth-friendly vehicles are on the rise.

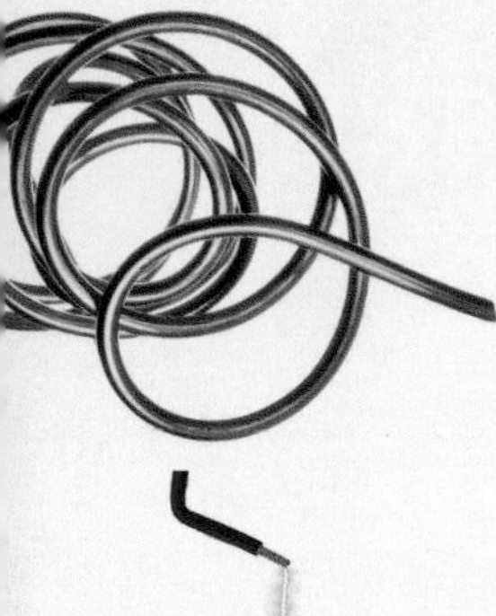

Conductor *(kuhn-**duhk**-tur)*

A substance that allows heat, electricity, or sound to travel through it.

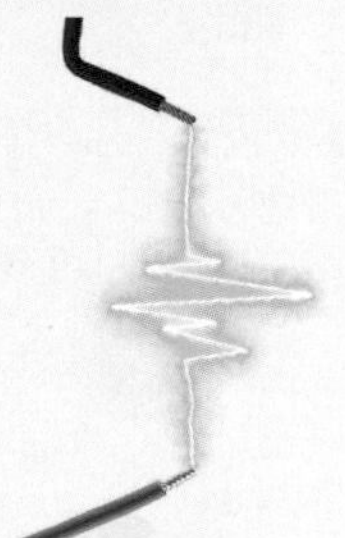

Electricity *(i-lek-**tris**-i-tee)*

Electric power that is generated in special, large plants and distributed through wires.

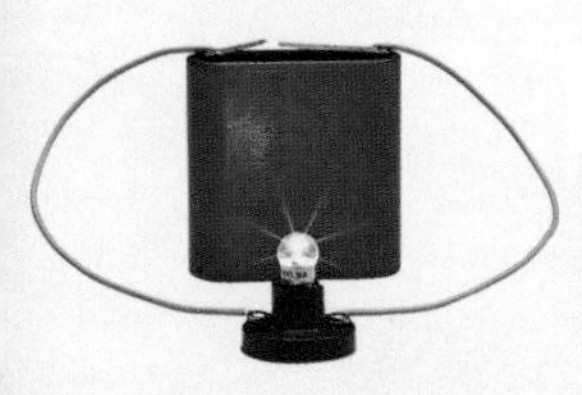

Load *(lohd)*

The part of a circuit that consumes electricity, like a light bulb or an appliance.

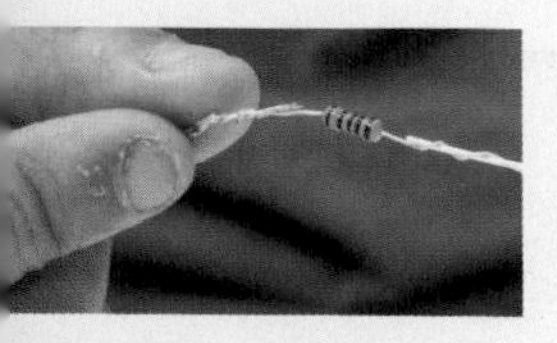

Resistor *(ri-**zis**-tuhr)*

The part of a circuit that reduces the flow of electricity.

INDEX

ABOUT THE AUTHORS

Kristina A. Holzweiss was selected by School Library Journal as the School Librarian of the Year in 2015. She is the Founder of SLIME—Students of Long Island Maker Expo and the President of Long Island LEADS, a nonprofit organization to promote STEAM education and the maker movement. In her free time, Kristina enjoys making memories with her husband, Mike, and their three children, Tyler, Riley, and Lexy.

Amy Barth is a writer and editor specializing in science content for kids in elementary through high school. She writes about robots, penguins, volcanoes, and beyond! She lives in Los Angeles, California.

Scholastic Library Publishing wants to especially thank Kristina A. Holzweiss, Bay Shore Middle School, and all the kids who worked as models in these books for their time and generosity.

Library of Congress Cataloging-in-Publication Data

Names: Holzweiss, Kristina A., author. | Barth, Amy, 1984- author.
Title: I can make exciting electronics/by Kristina A. Holzweiss and Amy Barth.
Description: New York, NY: Children's Press, an imprint of Scholastic Inc., 2018. | Series: Rookie star. Makerspace projects | Includes index.
Identifiers: LCCN 2017005025| ISBN 9780531234112 (library binding) | ISBN 9780531238806 (pbk.)
Subjects: LCSH: Electronics–Juvenile literature. | Science–Experiments–Juvenile literature. | Handicraft–Juvenile literature.
Classification: LCC TK7820 .H65 2018 | DDC 621.381–dc23
LC record available at https://lccn.loc.gov/2017005025

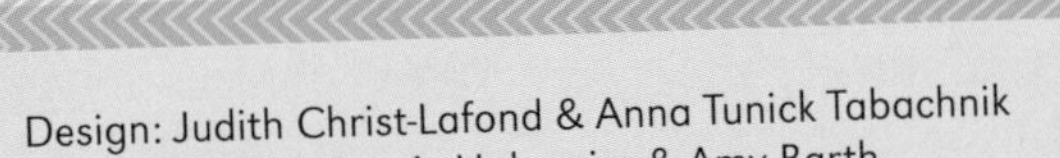

Design: Judith Christ-Lafond & Anna Tunick Tabachnik
Text: Kristina A. Holzweiss & Amy Barth

1 2 3 4 5 6 7 8 9 10 R 27 26 25 24 23 22 21 20 19 18

Photos ©: 6 scissors: fotomy/iStockphoto; 6 crayons: Charles Brutlag/Dreamstime; 6 tape: Carolyn Franks/Dreamstime; 6 glue gun: Nilsz/Dreamstime; 6 markers: Floortje/Getty Images; 6 straws: Olga Dubravina/Shutterstock; 6 marble: David Arky/Getty Images; 6 CD: Roman Sigaev/Shutterstock; 6 bottle cap: Mrs_ya/Shutterstock; 6 pencil: antomanio/iStockphoto; 9 background and throughout: Hugh-stoneian/Dreamstime; 9 wires: Westend61/Getty Images; 10 left and throughout: somchaij/Shutterstock; 12 bottom left: Antoni Bastien/Alamy Images; 15 light: BlackJack3D/iStockphoto; 21 circuit: Stephen Oliver/Dorling Kindersley/Science Source; 25 left: Bettmann/Getty Images; 25 center left: Thomas Abad/age fotostock; 25 center right: Ipsumpix/Corbis/Getty Images; 25 right: Stefano Bianchetti/Corbis/Getty Images; 26 left: Sarin Images/The Granger Collection; 26 top right: Stefano Bianchetti/Corbis/Getty Images; 26 bottom right: Science Source; 27 left: Tome & Life Pictures/Getty Images; 27 right: Culture Club/Getty Images; 28 left: Mary Evans Picture Library Ltd/age fotostock; 28 center left: Photo Researchers/Getty Images; 28 center right: Science Source/Getty Images; 28 top right: Oxford Science Archive/Print Collector/Getty Images; 28 bottom right: Ipsumpix/Corbis/Getty Images; 29 top left: SSPL/The Image Works; 29 bottom left: The Granger Collection; 29 top center: wolterfoto/ullstein bild/Getty Images; 29 top right: Chesky_W/iStockphoto; 29 bottom right: adventtr/iStockphoto; 30 top: Antoni Bastien/Alamy Images; 30 center top: Westend61/Getty Images; 30 center bottom: Stephen Oliver/Dorling Kindersley/Science Source.

All instructional images by Jennifer A. Uihlein.
All other images by Bianca Alexis Photography.